A

Vinyasa

of

Poetry

by

Jan Cumming

Published by New Generation Publishing in 2017

www.newgeneration-publishing.com

New Generation Publishing

This book is dedicated to

Sheila Baker, without whom it would never have started

All my Touchstone friends who have always encouraged
me to continue writing

&

For my three Mr C's - who make life complete.

Welcome to my book of words

That I have written over the years

Some may make you happy

Some may bring on tears

Some you may not understand

But then I don't know if I do

But hopefully in this book of words

They'll be something special for you

So when you think of poets who comes to mind? – William Wordsworth, Wilfred Owen, TS Eliot, Dylan Thomas, Carol Ann Duffy - I could go on. I was brought up on a diet of AA Milne, Edward Lear, Spike Milligan and Pam Ayres. So you can see my starting point. Like all works of literature different styles appeal to different people so I hope within this collection you find something that you enjoy and prompts some thought and emotion.

I am so pleased to be able to share this, my first collection of poems, with you all. I hope you enjoy the variety of poems that make up this compendium of my work. I started writing back in 2009 as part of a creativity course, Touchstone, which I did with a lady called Sheila Baker. I have been teaching Yoga since 2000 and I have been very lucky to have had some amazing teachers along the way. Sheila had taught me yoga for many years but was also a lecturer of design. Her belief in the use of art and design is infectious. She firmly believes that we all have a creative gene within us. I started the course thinking that

I could enter into some creative activity but trust me writing poetry was the last thing on my mind, so it came as a bit of a surprise.

I took some persuading about being a poet as I had always been a scientist at school. I was the Maths geek in my class. For me it was a perfectly straight forward subject. I adored it so much so I went on to do a degree in the stuff. However English was a completely different world. I could not understand the reasoning behind analysing a novel. It was either a novel you enjoyed or it was a novel that you did not enjoy. I found all the character observation and pinpointing key features of the plot a demanding puzzle to figure out. So much so that I got detention for doing my Maths homework in an English class. When the teacher asked me if I could concentrate on the novel at the same time as doing my Maths I did not help my cause by saying "of course". An hour of writing "I must concentrate in my English lessons" did not assist the situation. I have to admit I failed my English literature O level (that shows my age!) mainly because I answered the questions on Julius Caesar when we had studied Romeo & Juliet for the past two years. That was the rebel in me coming out, typically not to my advantage.

So when many years later I started writing poetry I was probably more shocked than anyone. But the more I wrote the more people engaged in my poetry. As a youngster I had always loved music and especially lyrics. I find I can recite most lyrics to most songs and I seem to learn them quickly. Seeing me dancing & singing along to the tunes on the radio, not always in tune but done with enthusiasm, is a common event in our house. So maybe it's not such a huge leap from lyrics to poetry.

I write about areas of my life that have had an impact on me – my family; illness that has afflicted those around me; adventures or experiences. Through my poetry I have also done some soul searching about myself and the demands of working and being a mother. I am not a traditional wordsmith and I hope that the words I use allow a clarity to my poetry that lets their power and emotion shine through.

So why a Vinyasa of Poetry? Vinyasa is a yogic term. In the tradition I teach in the lessons are constructed as a Vinyasa Krama – a special placement of postures in steps, so we prepare, have a main posture and then counterpose. If we break the word down Vi – means special, Nyasa means placement or gesture. So a Vinyasa of Poetry is a special placement of poems to focus your attention. Because it was Yoga that brought me to poetry it seemed the obvious title for my first collection. I sincerely hope that you enjoy the selection in this book.

Jan

Blessed

I must have done something that blessed me,

For I have truly been blessed

A trinity of love surrounds me,

A trinity that gives so much

A rock; stable and true

A golden arrow, passing through

And a beam of light, showing the way

What joy to be surrounded with each day

I must have done something that blessed me.

He

Crashing through the morning

Turning the clock around

Chaos become quite normal

Silence, seldom a sound

Pushing, Reaching, Trying

A river striving to find the sea

Frustration, Tears, Battles

Controlling the flood that was he

Breaking through the barrier

Now in charge of your fate

A giant appears before us

Calm, collected and GREAT.

Little Bean

Little Bean, your precious state

Releasing me from grief was your fate

A wise head, a young heart

Flashing away in the dark

The depths of the words

You sometimes impart

Sends messages deep within my heart

Your talents, your zest, the music you bring

Forget the grief, for now my soul can sing.

Change

Constant within our lives, yet resulting in the inverse for those involved

Happening around us, within us, to us each moment

Affecting our daily lives whether we realise it or not

Negotiating its meandering path; does fate define our pathway?

Generating a myriad of emotions and outcomes

Effectively the cause and reason of our evolution.

These next three poems were written when my father was suffering from cancer.

He was in his 70's when he was diagnosed with lung cancer.

The journey to his final day was a bumpy ride and I am sure many of you have been on similar journeys and know the emotions.

These are the poems it generated.

The Slug

It must have started before it began
The seed sown in the boy but grew in the man
The pillar of stone, crumbling from within
Emotions raw, smoking the sin.

The pictures so clear, the prognosis so bad
The battle commences, each triumph, we're glad
But cells gather pace and unite without warning
With trepidation we greet each morning

Radiotherapy, chemo and drugs
Soon the eye of the storm covers this slug
We live and forget what stays hidden deep
Waiting it's time to revive and to reap

And when it resurfaces, revealing its hand
All the onlookers can do is to stand
Sick to the stomach and trembling with fear
As the end of the pillar creeps ever so near

But still the pillar stands tall as before
His tears and despair hidden – no more
He will fight this battle on his own terms
Trying to make this slug squeal and squirm

Support and love, fear and laughter
We all dread what comes after
The pillar gone, but not forgotten
A wife distraught, can life be this rotten?

But death is where this journey ends
We go to meet our maker, to make amends
So should we harbour anger for the slug sent to see
How quickly he can reunite the man with Thee.

Give me

Give me your hands and I will guide you
As you travel through this forest so dark
Give me your arms and I will lift you
Too weak for the journey you must embark

Where is my sailor so strong and so true?
A constant protector, my emotional glue
Where is the parent who would carry this infant up to
bed?
Who put a sense of decency deep inside my head.

Where is the father who I looked up to so fondly?
Who taught me all he knew from a heart full of honesty
And where is the man I was honoured to call my friend
Taken away in this torturous end

So give me your body and I will carry you
Away from this fear and this pain
Give me your heart and I will love you
And in my heart you will always remain.

The Soul

I always thought the soul was the last to leave
But seeing you there I am not sure what to believe
Your shattered body struggling on
It seems your soul has already up and gone
Those eyes used to twinkle, a smile used to play
Your familiar face taken away
Replaced by a mask that tells of the end
But where is the soul in this body that won't mend?

Or maybe this is love's cloak of confusion
The soul is still there, what you see an illusion
Created so love can break the bonds so strong
And let your soul go travelling on
But why can't I see it deep in your eyes
Why do you wear this awful disguise?
I always thought the soul was the last to leave
But seeing you now I am not sure what to believe.

When my sons were young I worked in the computer industry and had to work away from time to time. Being a young mother there was always a sense of inner conflict. I was never really comfortable being away from them. So in the end I gave up computers to follow a new career teaching Yoga so I could fit it around them.....I never regretted my decision.

A Night Away

A night away with work or play
Away from the madness that is my normal day
Pampered and fed to my heart's delight
But somehow this luxury does not seem right

Out on my own, away from the nest
I really should be enjoying the rest
Removed from the chaos, the demands, daily chores
So why do I long for my own front door?

A comforting sofa, a night by the telly
Instead with haute cuisine I am filling my belly
But soon gaining information will require another
And I'll be back home, just being a mother

Do I want to progress? Do I want to move on?
But away from home always seems so wrong
To take what I know to a higher degree
Means stretching the limbic connection in me.

Corinne

A strength so deep coming from within

Responded to before the lights went permanently dim

A darkness surrounding the past months

Is gently broken...

But fearful, frightened, out on your own

Nothing belonging, no more home

These pages blank will fill over time

Drying your eyes....

A foreigner alone, in your land of choice

Depression receding, not given a voice

Spring will replenish what winter has stole

And you will blossom...

A new life will come to be found

Full of vitality, happiness, joy and sound

The decision made in the depths of despair

Will create light....

And you will grow

Tea Bag

The common tea bag, it must be said,

is not something to take to bed.

But given fresh in the morn, will lighten up

the darkest dawn.

And if presented by the one you love, will

be as good as turtle doves.

Energy

A moving hand
A closing eye
An inward breath
Energies rise

We begin to bend
Fold, melt, to move
Breath releases
Gentle and smooth

Practice replenishes
Energies within
Taken by the world
By stress? By kin?

Our breath fills us up
Our breath lets us go
Our energies ebb
Our energies flow

Yoga brings us to a point
Where do we wish to go?
Our energies balanced
For a moment or so.

Reflection

Concave, Convex, How do we reflect?

Do we bend or curve or see straight through?

Is our reflection the truth?

Or are we allowed the real you?

Revealed

Revealed at last the truth within

The inner light shines through the dim

Shadow of existence to show the true wealth

Hidden from myself

Please

Please don't turn out like your father
Know you are your mother's son
Please don't become detached from your offspring
And have no interest in whom they become

Know them as they emerge from childhood
Treat them as the adults we cannot yet see
I want them to know their father loves them
And that has to come from you not me

Please don't turn out like your father
It would bring me so much pain
The investment we have both made in raising them
Why lose all that we have gained

I know they sometimes drive you crazy
It is the old story of fathers and sons
But work to secure their friendship
So in years to come we can enjoy some family fun

Please don't turn out like your father
Pay attention to their lives
And if I should go before you
Please remember the words of your wife

Hands that touch

We sit facing, hand touching
We are aware of the binding of hot and cold
Our hands merge into one and we become aware
Of the slightest changes and movement
And all at once I am aware of your breath as well as my
own
Such a magnificent sensation
Feeling the inhale lift your ribs, sternum and shoulders
I can feel this in your hand
And then the exhale
The smallest of changes in fingers, palm, pressure,
connection
But a joyous experience I feel honoured to have shared

This is another poem inspired by my father's illness.

It was a hard day when he passed away.

He passed away on our wedding anniversary so the day always has happiness as well as sadness. I am sure he did not plan it but it makes the day easier.

Because of this combination it made me think about first love and how the joy of first love can so quickly turn to raw pain, when tears become daily currency.

Waterfall

A crystal clear waterfall falls silently from her eyes

As it descends to the earth the sun catches it and brings it to life

Each drop reflects the love given over so many years

As they fall towards the ground they take away her fear.

Cleansing the body, releasing the grief,

For a while this silent waterfall seems to give relief.

And love planted with tenderness as her life began

Will guide her through without this initial man

The waterfall will nourish seeds of love, hidden till now from sight

They will blossom and provide stability, despite this awful plight

And she will be filled with an inner love so strong and so deep

There will be no further need for her to sit and weep.

The Coat was written after a particularly difficult period in my life.

Someone I trusted deeply proved completely unworthy of that trust.

It was a complete surprise, I had not seen it coming and so was a huge shock and for a period turned my world a little bit upside down.

The Coat

I've been wearing this coat made from the most precious
threads

It's fine tapestry of colours mirroring the thoughts in my
head

It's kept me safe and warm, protected from the cold

But I fear now I must part with it, if I the truth I have been
told

It's taken me places, given me knowledge, opened my
eyes

But all along it seems it had a dark, more sinister side

It's been my faithful companion and I have handled it
with care

So what it now has done to me cannot be classed as fair

I believed this coat was made from the most pure natural
sources

However I now understand that it was woven by some
evil forces.

I don't want to have to throw my coat away

But now that I know these things how can it stay?

21

It's given me friends whom I love deep in my heart

For this reason alone I don't want us to part

But I am not the only one to be fooled by this weaver

A world of textiles from this fallacious healer

Precious threads now withered and torn

Colours washed out ready to mourn

The king's clothes have nothing on me

I have been wearing this coat and I still couldn't see.

Alarm

It's four forty A.M. in the still and the dark of the night
The moon is full, shining down in a glory of light
I stumble from my slumber and my feet meet the floor
I grab my dressing gown, ready to explore

I venture to the landing, my hearing piqued
Trying to discover which blessed smoke alarm squeaked
I slowly advance, listening out, towards its location
The cessation of this annoying sound my constant
motivation

It's the carbon monoxide alarm in the kitchen that's
calling
Why do these device's batteries always call for attention
before the day is dawning.
Resolved I shuffle back, under the duvet, looking for sleep
But my head is now full of thoughts, so I lie half wake until
the birds start to tweet.

Launde Abbey is a Christian Retreat House and Conference Centre set in some beautiful countryside in Leicestershire. I have been to many special Yoga retreats there over the years. It is set apart from the world, no mobile signal and originally no internet.

It is a beautiful space that allows you time for yourself and is where many of my poems have been written or inspired.

Launde

I've just arrived for another weekend of reflection
In a quiet spot tucked away from the world
And immediately I can feel each part of me relax and release
In the peace provided by Launde

I can connect with my creative side
Move, paint and write to my heart's content
I can recharge each and every battery within my soul
In the isolation provided by Launde

This act of stepping away from my busy life
Will provide me nourishment and insight
I will return to the world a better shade of me
Thanks to the love provided at Launde.

The Walk

We all decided to go for a walk one day

Magnificent views all along the way

Up and down the walk it undulated

But we agreed it was the coming down that we most
hated

On the way up our hearts did pound

But coming down just Thud, Thud on solid ground

The descent seemed to take us ages

At the end our legs felt like Jelly babies

Our knees were sore, ankles lost their strength

They just felt like jelly along their whole length

But we still hadn't reached the start

More walking required – now a completely different art

One foot in front of the other was all we asked

But our legs seemed unable to perform this simple task

They ached and wobbled and buckled at the knees

Simple extension and flexion now beyond our means

But still we had to struggle on

The path clear before us, we couldn't have gone wrong

And finally we finished, having followed all the orders

Don't know about the rest but tomorrow I want to be

fitted with better shock absorbers.

Mid life Crisis

Who am I and what do I wish?

So many roles, too many twists

Forward and backbend I bend, do I break?

Need to find answers, before my heart aches

I want to do this, I want to be that

But no one has written the following fact

I can't be all I wish, time will not allow

So I need to compromise, need to kowtow

Mother, wife, teacher, friend,

Daughter, gardener, cook, doesn't end

The roles I have, the roles I play

Will my dharma be clear one day?

So all I can do is follow the rules

Prioritise to fit within the schools

But maybe more important is just to be

Content and happy with the now that is me.

Space

Black holes are dark, white horses blue
Space around us is moving, Me? not a clue

Quantum mechanics, the atom so small
Space falling inward, under gravitational pull

A tiny mass, a massive weight
But what of man, are we clear of our fate?

Einstein stated relativity, a guide to the space around us
we see
But mix and match the whole world falls apart
Only to be left with the infinite part.

A tiny atom, a singularity
Back to the start with the big bang theory

Eucalyptus Tree

Standing tall and strong with a crumbling shell
The eucalyptus tree changes
Shedding its old dark skin to reveal its inner light
But is this transformation resisted

Old clinging to new, not wishing to be free
Where the two meet the creation of magical textures and
shapes
The eucalyptus tree stays the same
Just it's edges are cracking into a new form

Leaves flutter in the breeze, whilst the outer layer clings
on for dear life
Soon it will all be gone leaving the tree to glory in its new
disguise
Great sheets desperate to remain attached to the whole
Swaying in the vastness of space, their anchor
infinitesamally small

Nature allows us to witness the pain and beauty of this change
Observing the splitting of old from new, the minute interface between them slowly widening
In the created cracks and fissures, new life flows in, grows and evolves
And yet to some all they see is a eucalyptus tree crumbling and old.

So if this tree could speak, what would it say ?
Does it welcome this renewing process or mourn its shedding days
Does it wrestle with the change of identity from dark to light
Or does it relish the finish product and go and party through the night.

Yoga Philosophy tells us we are made of five layers – Body, Energy, Mind, our Personality & Emotions.

But we seem to be completely wrapped up in the first layer – our physical body?

When I was a teenager my friends and I always seemed to be on this or that diet and I feel the pressure on young people now is so much more intense than it was when I was that age.

The Body

We spend so much time fixated by this shell around our
soul
Comparing and contrasting, never aware of the whole
Why do we get encaptured by our physical formation?
When it is such a small part of our overall creation

Does it matter its shape or size, whether classed perfect
or not
We've all been given what we need, we should be happy
with our lot
And when we dig deeper into the layers beneath our skin
It's there we find the real treasures that allow our hearts
to sing

In February 2016 we received a phone call that all parents dread.

Our youngest son, who was 19 and away at university at the time, had been admitted to Coventry Hospital. His friend called us and it was like being in a bubble, time slowed down. We got into the car and drove the hour to Coventry. When we arrived he was wired up to various machines and had various drips in him.

He was diagnosed with Sepsis.

Thankfully it was caught early and he made a full recovery. All the staff at University Hospital Coventry were wonderful as was the Student Support at Warwick University. But special thanks go to his friends who were there when they were needed. And our thoughts are with those who don't escape Sepsis.

Six Foot Four

Six foot four of muscle lying useless on a bed

A pain of unparalleled proportions running around your head

Monitors attached to your chest, emergency drips inserted into your arm

There to warn anyone and everyone of any greater alarm

I sit and hold your pale hand, there's nothing else I can do

God I wish I could just scoop you up and cuddle you

But you're six foot four and far too heavy for me now to lift

And you're balanced on a precipice with death wanting to add you to its list

I've spent my whole life keeping you fed and watered, safe and warm

And now I find myself completely impotent, I can't control this storm

I'm just a spectator with my heart beating fast, stomach in my throat

Only to be consulted if you lose the ability to cast your own vote.

This infection microscopic, but its power flying free

I can watch it moving under your skin, contaminating with glee

Yesterday you were six foot four, fighting fit, so what went wrong

And now you're completely incapacitated, battling hard, God I hope you are that strong.

Nurses' shoes squeak as they walk around quiet night time wards

Antibiotics and morphine down tubes into your arms are poured

If I leave you, just for a moment, I feel such a tortuous physical ache

How many other families, right now, are encountering this same emotional earthquake?

Six foot four of muscle finally emerging from this fog

Seventy two hours of major medication seem to have done their job

We're allowed to take you home with more pills than we can count

Your name still on the land of the living headcount

I can't fully describe my feelings. I've been somewhere I never dreamt

I've clung on with my finger nails when it seemed everything was spent

We've been so very lucky, life has given you another chance

But think of those for whom this infection is their very last dance.

Motherhood

I've been a mum for over twenty years and boy has it
been great
Bringing up my two offspring has been such a glorious
fate
I have loved every single bit of it, the fun, the tears, the
laughter
But now that they are leaving home I wonder what comes
after?

All the effort I've put in has been leading to this day
When they will feel strong enough to start on their own
ways
But even though I have accomplished more than I could
ever have had wished
Their leaving is a bitter sweet pill and has an evil twist

It's leaving me feeling empty not knowing who I am or
where to go
I feel quite bereft. But I'm hiding it, it mustn't show
Has this void within me been there all my life?
Has it been covered over by being a mother and a wife?

So now's the time to tackle it. To find the I in me
And find the strength to journey into the unseen
So boys I hope that everything turns out the way you wish
If it doesn't I'll always be here to cook your favourite dish
And whilst you're out discovering your own individual
paths
I'll be at home exploring the way to my own heart

Sorry

Sorry I didn't have a lot to say

It's been a long week, long day

But when you're not here, to be connected over the air

It's just that I need to know you're there

I want to feel next to you

Even if there is nothing to say

But that is difficult when you are miles away

One day you'll be home to stay

I write a little poem for Christmas most years.

It's a time of year I normally enjoy but, in my mind, it has become increasingly commercialised.

But the other year with all the sad news around that commercial side seemed to be in complete contrast to what the world should be doing and this is the poem it created.

Note to Self

I don't know where to start this Yuletide rhyme
It's nearly Christmas Day and I'm running out of time
And I feel very different, this year, about the whole
Christmas thing
I'm trying to get enthusiastic but for me it's lost its zing.

We run around the high street or spend hours on the net
Buying presents no one particularly needs and running up
huge debt
We've become so obsessed with the idea of how
Christmas should be seen
We've made ourselves into every single advertiser's
dream.

But what is the real meaning of this festival that we mark
That should spread some joy and light amidst the winter
dark
And are we being true to that message and ourselves?
When we clear all the goods from the supermarket
shelves?

And what about those in our society less fortunate than
us
Do they benefit from all this commercial mush?
Or do they just continue to suffer what life has dealt to
them
Like the little baby boy born in a stable in Bethlehem

How do we allow ourselves to indulge in all this excess
and greed?
When there are people without roofs over their heads
with nothing on which to feed
And how do we feel when we unwrap presents that
apparently we crave
When just in order to survive some will hand over all that
they have ever saved

Is generosity providing those we love with more material
wealth?
At the expense of a sea of faceless strangers wellbeing
and health
And how do we celebrate the arrival of God's Only Son
In a way that reflects His love for us, each and EVERY one?

So this Christmas share fun and laughter with those you
care for
Cherish friends and neighbours – Go on Make a Fuss –
don't be a bore
But think about that baby and his life as it unfurled
And as Gandhi said "be the change you want to see in the
world"

Start with the little things that affect you every day
Think about the times you don't act on what you say
See if you can give to others things you actually NEED
yourself
And by all those little "going with outs" see if we can shift
a continental shelf

To a more peaceful world.

Tug of War

I think I am playing Tug of War
It's an internal form of the game
I can't decide whether to let my hair down
Or boot myself up the backside again

The ropes appear wherever I look
Each strand tugging me in different way
Confusion seems my normal state
My mind paralysed, so it can't have a say

Why so many choices?
Why no decisions made?
Why do I even have to think about it?
At this stage

My freedom beckons forward
My past won't let me move
My whole world has turned into a game
And I feel I might even lose

The ropes are getting thinner
Do I let them go or hold on tight
What I really could do with at this moment
Is some clarity and insight

I think I am playing Tug of War
It's not an easy game
I just hope that I can figure it all out
Before I go insane.

I wrote this poem about my decision to change my career.

The stress involved in day to day life seems to be endemic

So many of us are running just to keep up

Now I spend my time helping people move out of stress.

Division One

I have been playing in division one for as long as I can
think
Been keeping up with the best of them, in order that I
don't sink
But now I look at all there is, since all of this began
I have to admit that I really do class myself as an Also Ran

I've been keeping up with the Jones', getting the marks
that they demand
Been reliable and competent, too afraid to question
command
But where is the real me amongst all this frenzy,
competitive show
I'm putting in for a transfer to a division far below

I don't care if I am not at the top, just keeping my head
above water
I will be more comfortable in a lower league, no longer a
lamb to the slaughter
I can just be the me I want to be, no more part of the
struggle, the fight
And happily leave those in the top division to glory in
their own diffused spotlight

I won't worry if I succeed or not, won't reach for that
unobtainable goal
The journey has been endless, it's taken too much of a toll
I can be released from these shackles, no longer
imprisoned by what society requests
I can start to shed these personas, don't want to be like
all the rest.

I have been playing in division one for as long as I can
think
The stresses and the strains have nearly driven me to the
brink
But now I can cast that all aside and just enjoy my life
In a lower league where not winning is actually the prize.

Liberation

Liberation was the feeling, realisation was the pain
But even when I felt I had finally grown up, it ends in a moment of shame
Circles within circles, tangents left and right
Thinking I am in pure sunlight but ever present is the night

Child versus Adult, when will this equation be still
Thoughts in constant motion, not knowing what is your will?
I don't understand the polarity, to be so sure yet feel so unstable
I thought at last I could see ahead of me but stupidity makes me wonder if I'll ever be able

The speed is wrong, the accelerator stuck
The brakes not working, I see that much
But within the darkness my actions bring
Self-doubt and questioning are the constant sting

I need to know the answers, work this puzzle out
I should be calm and mature, so what makes me want to
shout
I need to grow up, to see the horizons beyond
I don't need these doubts holding me in their destructive
bond

Take a moment's stillness, flip the coin again
Stop the constant motion, spend some time within
This game plays around me – will it ever be clear
Do I just have to accept the falls and leap into the fear?

Arrows

Three, till you leave

Five, you'll no longer be home

I know that there will be some pain

But we will gladly fire you from our bow

You need to reach into your future

So that your own song you can sing

You've reached the time

When you no longer need our protective wing

We cannot come with you

You need to do this alone

But take with you the knowledge

If you need us we'll be here at home

You need to discover your identity

Explore challenging fields anew

But be sure the arrows that fire you forward

Will be coated with all the love you need to see it through

This is another poem written about the breakdown

of trust and how within an instant everything you felt

was solid is no longer there to support you.

What now?

I am falling but I don't know where

I am falling; it's as if I don't care

The bonds that have supported me along the way

Have been brutally and cruelly taken away

The trust I placed in those around

Lies shattered like glass on hard ground

I want to be still and catch my breath

This is so close to bereavement, to a death

But I must grasp the light amongst all this dark

Even if this episode leaves the deepest of marks

We dig through this field of glass with the sharpest of ploughs

But we come away cut and injured just thinking what now?

This poem was written when our sons had left home for university.

I am sure many parents know that feeling of the empty nest but it's not so much that it's empty as it changes the dynamics of home.

It's a time for adventure and opportunity for all but as parents you sometimes need to find out what it is to be a couple again.

Life's shapes

I started out as a plain sheet of paper, awaiting what was
to be
And each and every experience was written down, an
honest account of me
Whether good or bad, comic or sad, right or wrong
These scribbles on my paper were the beginning of my
song.

And life took me on adventures, whether away or at
home
And this plain sheet of paper took on a life of its own
The scribbles filled each inch of space, overlapping where
required
And I felt quite complete and happy, had all that I desired

Then along came another sheet with scribbles of his own
And before too long two become one and started up their
own home
And the sheets that started plain were joined for all to see
With a mortgage, joint bank account, and arguments as to
whose turn it was to cook tea.

These two flat sheets of paper that has started young and
bold
Were now formed into a tube of scribbles, secured by
bands of gold
And they planned on singing as a duet for a while, you see
But nature soon put pay to that and two became three

As time went along this triangle became the perfect
square
Four surfaces working together in a bubble of love and
care
Through the years this square developed into a multi
dimensional cube
Filled with all our experiences, laughter, tears and the
occasional boob.

As time went by this cube became our entire life
It encased us and absorbed us as we worked through our
daily strife
We started out with smiling little faces, bedtime stories,
grazed knees
And ended up with great big muddy rugby boots, exam
stress, "lend us a fiver please"

Our song became a crecendo so full of power and force
And sometimes in this mayhem I felt I had lost my voice
We worked with such lovely harmonies, with the
occasional discordant chord
But change was on the horizon, they no longer needed
bed & board

Then came the day when the cube just had to be divided
Two new plain sheets had to go, it was like they'd been
invited
To have their own adventures, the cycle of life repeats
But what now for our geometry? The cube was odd,
unstable, incomplete

The life that we've been through has been the greatest of blessings
But our shape now is uncertain, does it need a sterile dressing?
We're no longer that tube of scribbles, joined by bands of gold
We've been changed by so many things and in the meantime got quite old!

So what happens now? What shape does life become?
Whilst our offspring are away enjoying life, having fun
What shape is destined for you and for me?
How about some fun of our own – you any good at origami?

This next poem is about Anger.

We all encounter anger
from time to time but
how do we express that
anger?

Monster

There's a untamed monster living inside of me
It sits quietly, almost forgotten, biding its time to wake
But when the red mist descends or if life is threatening or unjust
It rises fiercely from below and creates an almighty fuss
This monster takes me down the paths that it has defined
Placing thoughts, words and actions into my mind
I fight with the courage, strength, tenacity of the beast
And I continue unabated until my enemies taste defeat

At the time I am possessed and filled with righteous indignation
And I have to confess that I truly enjoy the sensation
My words can wound but I don't really give a care
I just continue onwards, the monster permanently there.
But then the monster retreats from whence it has come
I find myself alone again, wondering "oh God what I have done?"
The actions others see are the monsters, not me
But others don't know of its existence, so this must be how I am seen.

I was completely convinced I took the right direction
But now am filled with guilt, did my actions need
correction?
It would not be so damaging if the monster was now dead
But with so many situations it raises its ugly head
I have to acknowledge this monster is just a part of me
But I don't seem able to control it, can't seem to see
A solution to the impact that this beast can bring
I need to find a way to keep it tethered in its ring.

Is it a weakness that allows the monster into my world?
Or do I encourage and feed it, willing it to be there
Do others have monsters that they manage to control?
Or are we all under the influences of internal beasts

And whilst the world is quiet and I know the monster
waits
What can I do to permanently quieten this fate?
How can I move forward and leave the monster behind
So others see me as I wish, polite and basically kind.

In memory of Peter

I'll fly above those monochrome mountains
I'll dive into those icy seas
I'll swim with whale song around me
And know that I am finally free

I'm no longer bound by that which held me
Painful for those I've left behind
But let my teaching fuel your creative juices
And just play and play and see what joys it produces.

To Elizabeth

We are faced with a barren field where we fear nothing
will grow
We stand frightened, immobile not knowing what to do
or where to go
Will anything prosper in this landscape set before you and
me?
How do we pick the fruit from a non-existent tree?

So let us plough this field with the tools we have at hand
Let us add an abundance of love and caring into this land
Then we can plant the seeds we find on our own
individual paths
And watch them germinate and grow and brighten up our
hearts

This barren field won't be with us for forever and a day
We are too unique and special for it not to have to change
It may be a hard journey but one day we will find
A beautiful flowered pasture that is yours and mine

And then we can both shine ---again

Vista

I see the vista of fields and hills stretch away into the
distant horizon
Tendrils reaching toward the mountains within
And wonder whether I could be transplanted into this
land
Would I flourish and thrive, spreading into the space
provided
Or would I become stunted, shrivelled, a foreigner in this
environment
The air here is clear, the sky so wide, the sea rolls into the
shore for mile after mile.
The sun illuminates each crystal of sand making the
beaches alive and vibrant with light, a halo edging the
ocean
The rocks have been shaped by millennia of movement
now seemingly fixed in their contorted shapes
The solidity of the ancient architecture telling tales of
times of conflicts and war
But now the wind just blows across tranquil fields of
wheat
Creating a soft symphony to accompany my footsteps
The barrenness of the landscape just adds to its beauty
This land refreshes and replenishes me, I feel so at peace
It embraces me, I feel welcomed into its fold
Or am I just tolerated?

Transition

How many of us walk around reflecting the white light
That shines and illuminates just a part of our might
Do we ever think of accessing the prism within?
That would allow each colour in us to spring

Transforming who we are, what we think, what we do
Allowing us to become a whole spectrum, not just the
glue
Letting us truly blossom from a deep untapped source
And so our Self can finally find its true unhindered voice.

Validity

If I look around at my friends and family, all of them, the
whole sum
I know the world would not be the same to me, without
just one
So why is it acceptable to believe?
The world could quite easily manage without me

I'm just as valid as all the rest
Whether or not I do my best
Whether the sky is grey or blue
I must somehow be important to all of you.

So why do I think I wouldn't be missed
I'd be forgotten as soon as an old shopping list
Where is the faith in my own self-worth?
Did it somehow get buried at birth?

Why is there a gap where my self-esteem should reside?
A void, a chasm, an emptiness deep inside
I knows others see me as whole, confident, complete
Oh, if they only realised I don't live in that elite

But this hole isn't there all of the time
There are days, months, years when I feel just fine
And then something shifts and I look to the floor
Only to discover – oh God – it's not there anymore.

But I'm the only one who can plug this gap
Who can build a well within me and top its cap
And from this well a love will fill me from within
And let my soul be ratified so I can finally sing

And then when the sound within me starts to increase
Maybe my doubting will finally cease
And I will see myself as others do.
And I will finally truly learn to love myself too.

Validity

Validity and Live Theatre are about how we can be so self-critical.

We can have such damaging internal chatter.

No matter how others see us and our qualities we ourselves can have internal conversations that convince us we don't have the same creditability as others.

Live Theatre

I am acting in a play, the play of my life
I am the star, it's my name up in lights
There are twists and turns to the plot, front of house
entranced
And there's a drop of sadness and a bit of comedy, if I get
the chance
The audience are mesmerised, caught up in my act
Carried off to a fantasy land, they don't care it's actually
fact
They are here to be entertained, to let go of their daily
woes
To just have an evening's fun, watching an incredible
show

But when the curtain lowers at the end of every night
I stand alone backstage, the audience beyond my sight
And whilst I hear them leaving with words of praise and
acclaim
I start my own inner conversation of criticism and blame
Why on earth do I bother? I am such a fraud
They must have sat there for hours being completely
bored
Why do I honestly think I can entertain a crowd?
As a classically trained actor, when I can only play a
clown.

What possessed me to believe that of this I could make a success?
They really can't mean all those kind words. It was a complete mess
So whilst the paper's reviews are glowing in their praise
My own interpretation is one of failure and of shame
But the show will continue, each day I'll give my best.
I'll keep getting up on stage, even if I think they could do with a rest
I'll persevere with my performance thinking one day I'll get it right
And allow my audience to be truly dazzled with my delights

But for years and years I have been acting in this play
And for so long it's that little voice within which has had to have its poisonous say
Then a spotlight illuminated my thoughts and I realised finally I have a choice
I can dismiss the negativity and listen to the positive voice
So maybe, just maybe the audience are actually right
For they see me in a completely different light
And so I find myself brave enough to allow my inner safety curtain to lift
And at last accept myself at my beautiful best and believe the words on their lips.

A visit to the Dentist

How badly I had prepared for my day in the dentist's chair

If only I had realised it would lead to weeks of despair

I thought I had it sorted, two days of invasive work

But I hadn't quite anticipated the results would drive me berserk

A clean and polish like I'd never had was what he promised me

After thirty years of perfect teeth where could the problem be?

Some bleeding gums, a case of plaque attacking where it could not be seen

A quick procedure would leave me with teeth I thought would gleam

I had mentally established myself for the needles and numbness he'd give

But how my mouth felt afterwards, I am still trying to forgive

My mouth no longer my own after this invasion

My gums, my teeth, my roots, my mouth shocked by this violation

For all my life my teeth had provided a stable mouth to feed

Their strength and ability to machinate had probably led to my greed

But now their strength and stability was rocked from within their base

Chewing became a problem, each individual food source a different case

A mouth that had known no problems was now so full of many

Sensitivity and sensations abounded in their plenty

My tongue surveys this strange landscape confused and trying to make sense

My eyes cry, my tears the only way I can show my offence

An earthquake has taken place within my oral den

My teeth and gums complaining, when will this end

Would time resolve this injustice, would time make it right?

When will I return to have my normal bite?

Many months have passed since then and finally I am free

From the pain and discomfort afforded to me

So what have I learnt from all this pain?

Well I won't be trusting that dentist again.

The Bible Rap

In Jesus' time, you couldn't shop online

When Noah conquered the flood, the NHS didn't want your blood

When Moses parted the waves, we weren't all YouTube slaves

And when God sent the tablets of stone, he didn't have access to a mobile phone.

During times with plagues of locusts and fleas, no one gave a damn about the Premier League

When Herod ordered all new-borns dead, no one envisaged one day babies would die 'cos their parents were smack-heads.

When David fought Goliath and won, skin cancer wasn't linked to time in the sun.

And when the Romans crucified Christ on the cross, were they talking of tax hikes and benefit loss?

When Jacob's coat of many colours was all the talk, you didn't have to be a size zero to make it onto the cat walk

When Mary gave birth in a stable bare, no one from the gossip columns could care

When Adam and Eve upset the apple cart, five a day wasn't linked to the health of your heart

And when Jonah was inside the whale, no one rushed to queue for the NEXT sale

When Daniel and the lion were to fight, animal rights campaigners were nowhere in sight

And when they wrote the book of Revelation, Strictly and X Factor weren't gripping the nation

So if you're today reading the Bible, don't dismiss it as libel

Even though it was written a long time ago. Do the stories still teach us things we need to know?

Traditionally in Yoga you do your first practice of the day when you first get up, sometimes at sunrise.

However I have never really been a morning person and a Yoga practice at 6:00/7:00am is not my ideal. Left to my own devices I get up, have a small breakfast and do my practice at about 8/8:30 am

So whenever I have been away on a yoga retreat those early morning practices have been a challenge. The quote from Hamlet "I think he doth protest too much" could have been said to be representative of my attitude. This next poem, Morning Practice, is dedicated to two of my wonderful teachers Gill & Karen as they have had to put up with their fair share of my complaining it was just too early. Thankfully the older I get the easier those early mornings are becoming, so there is progress

73

Morning Practice

I look around the room and see the serenity in their faces

They look so comfortable sat crossed legged in their places

So why do I feel disinclined to join in with this ritual

Is this anger I am promoting possibly becoming perpetual?

Have I become obsessed with creating my own raft of obstacles?

Allowed my ego to turn them into cherished personal trophies?

Presenting my case for the defence, just like a spoilt child

Would it be more honest to stamp my feet, throw a tantrum, however mild

What I need to do is wipe the slate clean, start with a fresh look

Stop re-reading this same chapter and create a new one in my life's book

Greet each morning with a slightly different choice

And allow those around me a rest from my whining voice.

So as of today I promise never to utter those words again

I will endeavour to participate, keeping my mind in this new frame

I will practice with an open heart; my eyes open to what they can see

But I wonder how long before I won't think "I would rather be in bed with a cup of tea"

The Serpent

A serpent of red, slinking into the night

White eyes, nowhere in sight

We sit, we wait, but not an inch do we gain

Hemmed in by metal and rubber, a huge automotive chain

Engines tick over keeping us warm whilst we're there

But this serpent is not for moving, where we need to get to, it doesn't care

So we sit, patiently in this excruciatingly long metal line

Just thinking it's probably worth taking the train next time.

This poem is about being stuck in a traffic jam on the M1.

It was late at night and we had travelled to Sheffield for a concert that was cancelled so we had to drive straight back home —not quite straight back as we spent 2 hours in the jam.

Brain

I think my brain is full

It's somewhat overloaded

Here comes more information

Oh no – it's imploded!!!

Cake

I made myself a Victoria Sandwich with flour, butter,
sugar & eggs

The sponge was light and fluffy and the jam inbetween
intense

I sprinkled icing sugar on the top to finish off my treat

Then came along my teenage son and all I have left is
cake crumbs at my feet.

Personality Change?

I need a personality change
Do you think it can be done?
I need to release from common sense
Have a little bit more fun
I need to take life less seriously
Worry a little less
Should I dye my hair a vivid pink?
Or go without a vest?

I need to have more faith in myself
Instead of harbouring all these doubts
Should I laugh at myself in the mirror?
Should I learn to scream and shout?
I need to be less organized
Arrive at places late
Should I rid myself of the watch on my wrist?
And just give myself up to fate

I could go out and leave the doors unlocked
I don't always need to be in possession of a first aid box
Should I learn to do a Moulin Rouge can can?
Instead of being old safe, reliable Jan
Should I stop writing complaint letters?
Should I groove to the latest beat?
Should I let myself run naked around the village?
Instead of always wearing something sensible on my feet.

Do I always need to count my pennies, making sure the sums add up?
Could I drink my tea from the saucer instead of using the cup?
Should I give up all hope of ever again being a size 12?
Should I wonder if in my garden there are pixies and elves?
I need a personality change
Do you think it can be done?
I need to turn around the years
And let my face enjoy the sun.

If change were .....

If change were like my brother
You'd know when it had arrived
You'd be knocked off your feet sideways and transported
on a ride you'd be lucky to survive
Along with all the chaos that it would inevitably bring
you'd have masses of fun and frolics and time to shout
and sing
But along with all the laughter – you'd be mighty glad for
the rest after

If change were like my mother
It would come with a constant narration
It would change its direction on a whim and leave you
stranded in utter frustration
You'd spend more time chatting to strangers than making
headway along your path
But somehow you would not mind as this change would
be like a lovely friend, with a very big heart

If change were like my father
Wow betide the ones that failed
Once on the course determined no U-turns are to be
availed
Stiff upper lip and backbone are required to stay the
course
And if necessary you'd be dragged through backwards,
like a plough behind a shire horse

If change were like my sons
It would be handsome, tall and strong
But for some unfathomable reason couldn't stay upright
very long
It would need to lie down, head supported, with an
electronic device in its hand.
Be communicating in the ether; nourishment needed, is
this change you could stand?
It would be incredibly user intensive as it passed through
your life
But its joy, potential and energy would somehow negate
all of this strife

If change were like my husband
It would stay the course of time, be patient and
determined and supportive along the line
It would not waiver from its charter as it steered you
along the way, would know what and what NOT to say
It would be kind and protective, the sweetest form of
change
But alas would come with a very large dose of TV Sports,
which might leave you somewhat deranged

And if change were like me
It might not be too exciting
It would be constant and loving; so possibly quite inviting
It may be done in a rush, so you could fit a bit more in
And would no doubt involve a walk, to clear the clutter
within
But when all the change was sorted and finally done
You could sit down with a cup of tea and a lovely
homemade bun.

Why does my nose run?

It is winter and I have the obligatory cold. Which let's face it isn't fun

And I am taking all the correct medication but tell me

Why does my nose still run?

Last week it was so well behaved. Just sitting on the front of my face

And now it's like a river delta in flood

Leaving nothing in its wake

I go out to clear my head. Maybe the cold will allow my snout to cease

But no, as soon as the fresh air touches my nostrils it's like a spring

Will there never be nasal peace.

It dribbles and pours, I sniff and snuffle.

This hooter of mine is causing a whole load of trouble

From my beak falls the most amazing cascade?

And one thing is for certain it's all man-made.

My proboscis has taken on a life of its own.

Maybe I could find it another home.

But the element that really makes me want to cry

Is it has the audacity to do this right in front of my eyes.

So if you too are suffering from a leaky schnozzle. And
your world is very damp

My advice to you is quite simple

Go out and buy a great big clamp.

Breaking In

I feel that I am breaking into my shell
But I'm having to use a pneumatic drill
As it's really quite difficult and resistance is all around
And the drill doesn't help as it makes a bloody awful
sound

But just when I think I can no longer fight the conflict
The shell starts to give way, just a little chink
Allowing me a glimpse of the unfettered joy that's within
So I'll have to keep drilling and just accept the din.

This chink shows me there's another way through the
turmoil
My self needs a really good service, M.O.T. and oil
And being surrounded by others and given the space
I can set about breaking the shell and bringing a smile
back to my face.

So let me loose with this pneumatic drill

Put on your ears defenders, I'm going in for the kill

The joy within will guide me through the transitions that I face

And replace the frustrations and angst with joy, laughter and grace.

Post !

My post has gone missing; I don't know where it is
There are certain things in transit that I am starting to
miss
I ordered some coloured twine just the other day
The seller sent me an email: "it's on its way"

But five days later and not a hint of arrival
I don't need it till next month, it's not vital for my survival
But where can it be, why's it taking so long.
There should be two lots of concert tickets as well-
what's gone wrong?
And the books I ordered that are travelling through the
ether
Yep, you've guessed it, haven't got them either

There's a new postie this week, young & innocent he
looks
I wonder if he has a secret stash that includes my tickets
and my books
Or maybe he is just confused between 10 and 10A
And my post has gone to my neighbour's for a holiday

Or maybe it's someone in the sorting office that is holding
up my delivery
Maybe I should have asked the senders to put it in Royal
livery
I have received all the junk post – you know the ones that
go straight into recycling
But nothing of any consequence seems to be arriving!!!

So where is my post? Where can it be?
And why do these things always happen to me?
There's a tube of glue and ceramic paint, that are
somewhere in a jiffy bag awaiting their fate
They should have fallen through my letter box to my hall
floor
But it seems neither have even been close to my door

So who in Royal Mail is responsible for this delay?
According to customer services I have to wait 3 weeks for
them to say.
Ahhh there's half a dozen light bulbs that I must receive
They were supposed to go to my mums so pleaseeeee
Let them arrive safely with all my other clobber
And then my life can continue without this endless bother

A new day arrives and here comes that young postman
With all my post I am surprised he is not in a van
And then through the letterbox a cascade of letters and
small parcels fall

Problem as always – I've no patience at all.

Christmas Snow

A beautiful little snowflake falls gently from the sky

Another softly flutters down and lays by its side

And quietly on Christmas Eve all snowflakes there do gather

To make the scene on Christmas Day a wondrous winter platter

Presents and treats are forgotten as we rush to explore

Coats and gloves and wellies are hurriedly put on as we go through doors

Into this land of snowflakes, oh what a marvellous sight

That's silently laid itself down for us during the dark of the night

Our footsteps are muffled and a hush pervades around

Children's laughter and shrieks are the dominant sound

Nature has wrapped itself up in a beautiful blanket of white

Providing us with a banquet of fun that will entertain us till twilight

And when we have played to our heart's content
And snowballs have been thrown, maybe the odd tear
been shed
When our hands are cold and numb from the snow
We will be filled with a joy, we don't often know

Each unique snowflake contributes to the scene
And makes us realise how simple happiness can be
It brings an element of innocence back into our life
Allowing us to let go of daily stresses, worry and strife

So whatever your Christmas holds for you this year
Take a moment to know what and who you hold dear
And treasure the simple things in life that make it worth
living
And know Christmas is about simply loving and giving

I think

I think I'd like to be a cat
And sleep all day on a cosy cushion or mat
Or should I rather be a tree
And blow around in a hurricane or just a gentle breeze
Or I could even be a book
And teach people about places, tell them stories, let them cook
Or I would rather be a car
And zoom along motorways and travel so far
Maybe I could be a vast star in the night
Shining brightly down on the world with all my might
But then I think I'd like to be a worm in the soil
Creating a fertile land for crops with all my toil
Or maybe I could just be the air
And float around without a care
But, NO, I think that I should just be ME
Because that's what the world needs me to be.

Redundant

My husband's been working for the same company for years and years and years

And they've given him redundancy, it's a case of cheers rather than tears

We might struggle financially but with prudence we should cope

And at last that company will no longer have my husband by the throat.

So now he's on 3 months gardening leave. He's not allowed to be employed

So he's going to become my Haus Frau – I'm sure he's overjoyed.

He's going to be my personal barista, cleaner, cook.

I'm sure we'll soon be singing from the same hymnbook

So he brings me a cup of tea with the morning sun

And smiles as he says "yes Darling I'll fit the odd job in when the summer cricket's done!!"

I have reach the menopause.

JOY!

A time in a woman's life when her body can react in a myriad of ways that she has no control over or idea about.

My body now reacts to alcohol, so that lovely glass of wine at the end of a busy day with a meal is now a little bit like Russian roulette.

So came about Just One Glass.

Just one Glass

I can sense it coming in the distance
Its source is quite unknown
I can feel it gathering intensity
Will it never leave me alone?

I can almost smell this monster
Straight from the fires of hell
Creeping up upon me, when it'll
Pounce no one can tell

It's like trying to escape a volcano's
Pyroclastic flow
Running away from the heat of a
Forest fire's glow

But I know I can't escape it
It will always find me out
It just comes upon me with
Such ferocity and clout

My skin starts to prickle
With the fear of what's ahead
My forehead starts to perspire
My palms clammy with dread

It feels like I'm in a furnace
Surely I'm going to melt
The temperature is just rising
Like the heat from a speeding meteor freed from the
asteroid belt

So what is this monster breathing down my neck?
This thermodynamic blast that leaves me just a wreck
I only had one small glass of wine not a pint of triple sec.
But here it comes - another blessed hot flush – oh heck

If I .....

If I were to die tomorrow, if I were to pop my clogs.

Don't feel sad or sorrow, I've been happy with my lot.

I've led an exciting life, though my bucket list is not complete.

But the things on there are quite expensive, so maybe it's better if I'm deceased.

If I were to die next week, if I were to finally kick the bucket.

Don't shed a tear, I know a funeral was not in our current budget.

But please ensure when I'm taken to that final ceremony, to find out heaven or bust

I'm not in a slow hearse, holding up traffic, let me go in the fast lane with some V8 thrust

If I were to die next month, shuffled off this mortal coil.

Put a smile on your face, don't let grief make you toil.

Don't become a coffin boffin with your every conscious thought at my grave.

Let your mind see me walking the hillsides, taking in the sunshine, enjoying the waves.

If I were to die next year, if my number was finally up.

Don't forget all our memories, all the fun, the laughter, the mishaps.

Cherish what we had together, remember when we laughed till the tears ran down our faces

All the travel we did and the magical experiences we had in those far flung places.

But If I'm lucky enough to live to a ripe old age

Don't let me take my time for granted – let's have a rave

Let our life be adventurous, be foolish, let's take some risks, become illustrious

So when I finally do go I'll be content, without fear, ready to turn to dust.

The Sparrowhawk's Week

Fancy a nice chaffinch, as they seem to eat the most

Maybe I could bag one for my Sunday roast

And then on Monday something quite quick

Possibly a little house sparrow on a spicy kebab stick

Swallow stew on Tuesday but there is no need to boast

On Wednesday I'll be happy with robin red breast on toast

Thursday – well I might have to cease

One doesn't want to be labelled obese

But back to work on Friday, no rest for the wicked

I'll swoop into number 6 and grab a great fat pigeon

They're quite a job to skin you know, but worth the extra work

As they'll satisfy my appetite and with the feathers I can do my own Damian Hurst

That just leaves Saturday, the end of my week

I fancy something that used to go tweet

I could have blackbird curry or tapas with wren

Or maybe a magpie or a flipping big hen

Whatever I decide there is one thing to know

When you are top of the food chain – anything goes.

This poem is dedicated to Pam Ayres. I went to see her in Newark and she said the first line but then declared she had got no further, so I went home and completed my own version. I hope she would be happy with the result but I'm sure she could probably improve on them.

WNGD

Saturday the sixth of May

Was world naked gardening day

So the question that came to my mind

Would having no pockets be a bind?

And where could I secure my trusty clippers?

I certainly could not stuff them, as normal, down my knickers

And how would I carry all my packets of seeds?

Under my ample cleavage or could I wedge them between my knees?

But never one to fall at the first fence

I ventured out in the buff hoping I would not cause offence

My old gardening clothes stayed sadly on the floor

But I was totally liberated - I did not need them any more

However a passing spectator would probably have difficulty to see

If there were more creases on my those old clothes or me

But I just grabbed my fork and spade

Happy to enjoy some digging as God intended me to be made.

I pruned, I trimmed, I weeded and I planted here and there

I mulch around my precious buds taking care of their welfare

I decorated the garden bed with a selection of pebbles and stones

And picked up some collateral damage around my crumple zones

The birdlife weren't upset at all by my lack of attire

Mind you that upset with the pyracantha bush certainly made my voice go higher

And the squirrels still scurried around my water butts

Again no problem as thankfully I don't contain nuts.

So my garden at last received the attention it deserved

Hopefully in private and completely unobserved

As it's not a good look for cutting the grass and pulling up old roots

Just wobbling naked flesh finished off with wellington boots

But it's quite enlivening to be free from all restraints

And so far there have been no comments or thankfully complaints

But I think next time I go out to deal with my roses and my heather

I'll be making a point of demanding some much warmer weather.

My last poem in this collection is to my teacher Sheila.

On many occasions I have attended her Yoga retreats and have always come away refreshed. Normally we have an art session during the weekend so you leave with a piece of artwork under your arm you probably did not even think you could produce.

She inspires many people.

Sheila

How do we say thank you for everything you bring

You tempt us back each and every year. You get us to write, paint and sing

You plan our physical movements so our mind and breath expand

You teach us so beautifully, we can all sense Peter's guiding hand

You test and tease and challenge us with acrostics and haikus

We wouldn't put up with it from anyone else – except you

You allow us to discover where our true Self resides

And you look after us if we have enquiring minds, questioning hearts, tired or tearful eyes

And over the weekend we transition due to your teaching

It's either that or just because we do so much eating

But most importantly you make us realise how special we all really are

But that's because we reflect the light from our wonderful Yogic Star.

Alphabetical Index of Poems

Lightning Source UK Ltd.
Milton Keynes UK
UKOW05f0412300617

304364UK00003B/100/P